GET INVOLVED!

HUMAN RIGHTS ACTIVIST

POWER to the PEOPLE

Be a Junior Activist

Ellen Rodger

Crabtree Publishing Company
www.crabtreebooks.com

D0004490

Crabtree Publishing Company

www.crabtreebooks.com

For today's activists, who need to know and remember the past in order to make a better tomorrow.

Developed and produced by Plan B Book Packagers

Author:
Ellen Rodger

Art director:
Rosie Gowsell-Pattison

Editor:
Carrie Gleason

Production Coordinator:
Margaret Amy Salter

Crabtree Editor:
Molly Aloian

Crabtree Proofreader:
Adrianna Morganelli

Photographs:
David Hancock/Alamy: front cover
Dreamstime: Ankevanwyk: p. 19
iStockphoto: Chris Schmidt: p. 11
Shutterstock: luminouslens: cover (paper); Sergei Bachlakov: p. 1, 18; Roadk: p. 3; Helen & Vlad Filatov: p. 4; Benjamin F. Haith: p. 5; Catherine Jones: p. 6; Ken Brown: p. 7, 10 (left); Morgan Rauscher: p. 8; Simone van den Berg: p. 9; riekephotos: p. 10 (right); Keith Brooks: p. 12 (bottom); Juha Sompinmäki: p. 12 (top); Philip Lange: p. 13; LouLouPhotos: p. 14; Ronen: p. 15; Paul Cowan: p. 16 (bottom left), 17; Sam DCruz: p. 16 (bottom right), 24; Zack Frank: p. 20; shae cardenas: p. 21 (top); Sylvana Rega: p. 21 (bottom); Dhoxax: p. 22 (top); Paul Prescott: p. 22 (bottom); ARTEKI: p. 23; Steve Estvanik: p. 25; Ken Brown: p. 26; Benny Gool: p. 27; Yuri Arcurs: p. 28 (top); Lisa F. Young: p. 28 (bottom); Andresr: p. 29 (bottom); Elena Elisseeva: p. 29 (top); Elise Gravel: p. 30-31; Crystal Kirk: p. 31 (bottom)

Cover: A young girl attends a candlelight vigil at a rally against the death penalty.

Title page: Protestors with handmade signs gather together as one group on the steps of a public building.

Publisher's note to teachers and parents
Although careful consideration has been made in selecting the list of Web sites, due to the nature of the subjects' content some Web sites may contain or have a link to content and images of a sensitive nature. The views and opinions presented in these Web sites are those of the organization and do not represent the views and policies of Crabtree Publishing. As Web site content and addresses often change, Crabtree Publishing accepts no liability for the content of the Web sites.

Library and Archives Canada Cataloguing in Publication

Rodger, Ellen
    Human rights activist / Ellen Rodger.

(Get involved!)
Includes index.
ISBN 978-0-7787-4695-9 (bound).--ISBN 978-0-7787-4707-9 (pbk.)

    1. Human rights workers--Juvenile literature. 2. Human rights--Juvenile literature. 3. Human rights--History--Juvenile literature. I. Title. II. Series: Get involved!

JC571.R63 2010   j323   C2009-901930-2

Library of Congress Cataloging-in-Publication Data

Rodger, Ellen.
    Human rights activist / Ellen Rodger.
       p. cm. -- (Get involved!)
    Includes index.
    ISBN 978-0-7787-4707-9 (pbk. : alk. paper) -- ISBN 978-0-7787-4695-9 (reinforced library binding : alk. paper)
    1. Human rights--Juvenile literature. 2. Human rights workers--Juvenile literature. I. Title. II. Series.

JC571.R657 2010
323--dc22
                                              2009013336

Crabtree Publishing Company

www.crabtreebooks.com   1-800-387-7650

Published in Canada
Crabtree Publishing
616 Welland Ave.
St. Catharines, ON
L2M 5V6

Published in the United States
Crabtree Publishing
PMB16A
350 Fifth Ave., Suite 3308
New York, NY 10118

Published in the United Kingdom
Crabtree Publishing
White Cross Mills
High Town, Lancaster
LA1 4XS

Published in Australia
Crabtree Publishing
386 Mt. Alexander Rd.
Ascot Vale (Melbourne)
VIC 3032

Contents

GET INVOLVED!

What are human rights?

Human rights are the basic rights that all people are **entitled** to. These include the rights to life, freedom, and equality. These rights, and many others should not be denied to a person based on their race, religion, gender, abilities, political opinion, or age.

Does the idea of people being beaten, imprisoned, or killed for their beliefs upset you? Would you be shocked to learn that slavery still exists in some parts of the world today? If so, then human rights might be something you will be interested in learning about.

No rights?

There are places in the world where people are tortured or killed because of who they are or what they say. They are jailed or **discriminated** against. They are forced into slavery because someone else needs cheap labor. When these things happen, we all suffer and become less human.

An activist stands up and speaks out for those who cannot speak for themselves, either because they are in prison, fear for their safety, or cannot speak freely.

4

Humans have dignity!

Human rights are about recognizing that all humans have **dignity** and should be respected no matter who they are, where they came from, or what they do. The definition of human rights is constantly **evolving**, and the struggle to protect them is a continuing fight. Activists are people who care. They are people who constantly work to gain and protect human rights.

BIG MOUTH

Get Active!

Human rights—what are they?

Do you know what your rights are? In many countries, people are guaranteed basic rights in a constitution or a bill, or charter, of rights. Bills or charters of rights are often written documents. They protect the rights to free speech, thought, expression, religion, association, and freedom of the press. They often also prohibit the government from actions that are cruel. All freedoms come with responsibilities. Freedom of expression means being able to speak freely without censorship. It does not mean a person can say things that are proven to be untrue or that express hatred toward another person or group. Do some investigating to find out about your country's constitution and rights documents. Find out what your freedoms are.

Once you know what your freedoms are, speak out to protect them!

What is an activist?

An activist takes action to make things better. A human rights activist is someone who supports and speaks out for others when they cannot speak for themselves. Anyone can be an activist. All you have to do is care, become informed, and learn everything you can about an issue.

What do they do?

Activists do their work in different ways. Some are educators who inform others about human rights. Others work or volunteer for organizations that promote their cause. Many write letters to politicians and governments in the hope that they will listen and act on pleas for help. Human rights activists do everything from raising funds to marching in protests and boycotting businesses and governments that abuse human rights. These kinds of non-violent acts are called "direct action." These peaceful demonstrations and protests bring attention to an activist's cause.

These anti-war activists are marching in a parade. Sometimes it is not easy to be an activist, especially if people are against your cause.

Field Notes:

American **civil rights** leader Dr. Martin Luther King, Jr. was famous for his inspiring speeches and for using non-violence when fighting for human rights. His "Letter from a Birmingham Jail" was written while he was jailed for protesting in 1963. He explained that it was his **moral** duty to disobey laws that were unjust and did not respect human rights. In this passage, he explains the purpose of direct action:

"You may well ask: "Why direct action? Why sit-ins, marches and so forth? Isn't negotiation a better path?" You are quite right in calling for negotiation. Indeed, this is the very purpose of direct action. Nonviolent direct action seeks to create such a crisis and foster such a tension that a community which has constantly refused to negotiate is forced to confront the issue. It seeks so to dramatize the issue that it can no longer be ignored...

My friends, I must say to you that we have not made a single civil rights gain without determined legal and nonviolent pressure. Lamentably, it is an historical fact that privileged groups seldom give up their privileges voluntarily... We know through painful experience that freedom is never voluntarily given by the oppressor; it must be demanded by the oppressed."

Dr. Martin Luther King, Jr. spoke out for the rights of African Americans.

Why should you care?

Uniting together at a protest sends a powerful message.

There are many reasons why people should care about humans rights. These rights affect us all. If we don't care about others, who will care about us? Caring about others means building communities of respect and acceptance.

Human rights belong to everyone. Sometimes people who have many rights and freedoms forget that other people's rights are being denied.

Don't just sit there!

Human rights activists have learned that doing nothing protects human rights abusers. Activists do not wait on the sidelines and watch while people are being harmed. They believe they have to act! Actions can be as small as speaking out or as large as organizing a rally.

Human rights violations—what are they?

The fight to end slavery was a fight for human rights. Owning humans was not considered wrong in much of the world 150 years ago. Today it is considered a human rights violation around the world. Torture, **detainment**, arrest, and **exile** are common human rights violations. Other examples of human rights violations are:
– Denying people the right to express their opinions
– Not allowing people political rights, such as the right to vote
– Preventing people from traveling freely in and out of the country they were born in (a right of citizenship)
–Withholding the right to education and equal protection under the law

Get Active!

Shopping for human rights

One way to show you care about human rights is to refuse to buy products produced in a sweatshop. A sweatshop is a workplace or factory that pays workers poorly, makes them work long hours, and does not treat them well. Sweatshops produce cheap goods by exploiting people. Some sweatshops use young children as workers. Others do not allow workers to take breaks. If they hurt themselves at work, workers are often fired. A T-shirt produced in a sweatshop may be cheap to buy but it comes at a high cost to human rights.

Here are some simple ways to stop supporting sweatshops:

- Check the label on goods before you buy. If the tag says "union made," it is more likely to be produced in a workplace that pays a reasonable wage and respects workers' rights.

- Shop at stores that publicly refuse to carry sweatshop-produced goods.

- If possible, buy handmade. People who make and sell their own goods such as clothing or toys can set a price that fairly reflects the work required to make them. This means shopping at venues such as craft markets.

Go to the mall and check the stores there to see where the items they carry are made.

Declaring human rights

In 1948, the world was still recovering from the horrors of **World War II**. The cruelty, death, and mass murder of the **Holocaust** forced people to examine human rights. People asked: how could this have been prevented and how can we make sure it never happens again?

THE HOLOCAUST 1933-1945
L'HOLOCAUSTE

Canada 45

Millions of people died during the Holocaust. The UN Declaration of Human Rights had its roots in the desire to never let this happen again.

Doing it right

After the end of World War II, the **United Nations** was created. It passed the first Universal Declaration of Human Rights as a way of saying human rights are important and all countries have a responsibility to respect them. The declaration combines political rights with cultural, social, and economic rights.

The declaration was signed by many countries, but that did not mean human rights were magically protected. The declaration is a tool used to urge countries to "do the right thing." A country that has signed the declaration but denies rights to its citizens is put under pressure by the UN and other countries. Pressure can be in the form of economic punishments such as denying trade or applying **sanctions**, or penalties.

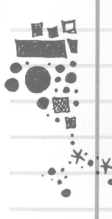

Field Notes:

The Universal Declaration of Human Rights was the first declaration of the rights that all humans are entitled to and includes 30 articles, or statements of rights. A few are listed here:

Article 1: All human beings are born free and equal in dignity and rights. They are endowed with reason and conscience and should act towards one another in a spirit of brotherhood.

Article 2: Everyone is entitled to all the rights and freedoms set forth in this Declaration, without distinction of any kind, such as race, color, sex, language, religion, political or other opinion, national or social origin, property, or birth.

Article 3: Everyone has the right to life, liberty and security of person.

Article 20: Everyone has the right to freedom of peaceful assembly and association.

Get together with a group of friends. Discuss how the declaration protects your rights.

This picture shows some of the skulls of people murdered by the Khmer Rouge government in Cambodia from 1975 to 1979.

A marker at a mass gravesite in Cambodia where this crime against human rights occurred.

Not enough

Declarations are good, but they are not enough to ensure human rights are protected. Sanctions and shame are sometimes not enough. Often the only solution is to send United Nations peacekeeping troops out to protect people. This can be a long process. The UN has a Human Rights Council which reviews human rights records in the 192 countries that are UN members. But action on human rights is often slow.

Setting standards

The UN Declaration has helped define human rights—an important first step. Many other declarations and laws protecting rights have come about since 1948. The UN Declaration has also helped set standards of treatment for people such as prisoners and **refugees**. Article 5 states that "No one shall be subjected to torture or to cruel, inhuman or **degrading** treatment or punishment." This means that it is a human rights violation to treat people inhumanely, even if they have been convicted of a crime. Article 14 states that "everyone has the right to seek and to enjoy in other countries asylum from persecution." This means that people have the right to seek freedom in another country if they fear attack for who they are.

This is the UN headquarters in New York. The UN was formed in 1945 as an international organization that works for peace and justice.

In the beginning

Other treaties and declarations have their beginnings in the UN Declaration. In 1969, the American Convention on Human Rights was adopted by countries in the Americas. Similar conventions were adopted by European and African countries. Conventions are legally binding. This means that countries that sign them must abide by them. People who feel their rights have been violated can take the country to court.

Get Active!

Learn about the UN Declaration

Human rights declarations and conventions are often used to pressure people, groups, and countries into respecting rights. To find out what rights the United Nations' Universal Declaration of Human Rights protects, check out the UN Web site and print out a copy. Read it and look up difficult words and concepts in a dictionary. Becoming informed is one of the first and most important steps an activist can take. You can download and print the UN Declaration from the United Nations Web site: www.un.org.

Right to be free

The fight to end slavery was one of the biggest human rights struggles in history. Abolitionists were activists who were morally opposed to slavery. In the late 1700s, British abolitionists began speaking out against the use of slaves on British-owned plantations in the Caribbean. They interviewed slaves and gathered evidence that slavery was **barbaric**. This material was used to convince people that slavery was wrong. Eventually, the abolitionists won politicians over to their cause and a series of laws were passed in Britain and its colonies, ending slavery there by 1833.

Activists' tactics

In the mid-1800s, abolitionists in the United States adopted similar tactics to end slavery. They spoke out at public meetings and published newspaper articles and letters. They also worked on what would today be called direct action causes such as the Underground Railroad, a secret network of people who helped slaves escape to freedom in Canada. It took the **Emancipation Proclamation**, a civil war, and the **Thirteenth Amendment** to end slavery in the United States in 1865.

This memorial statue on the Detroit River commemorates the Underground Railroad.

Slavery still exists!

Did you know that slavery still exists? Some human rights organizations believe that almost 30 million people around the world today are slaves. They are forced to work without pay and are beaten or tortured when they resist.

Fighting slavery

Article 4 of the Universal Declaration of Human Rights states that "no one shall be held in slavery or servitude and that slavery and the slave trade shall be prohibited in all their forms." Human rights activists fight slavery today through education and rescue campaigns.

BIG MOUTH

Get Active!

Join the fight—become an abolitionist

How can you help prevent slavery? Today's anti-slavery activists use many of the same tactics they did in the 1800s. They organize events to publicize the fact that slavery still exists. They educate, communicate, and raise funds. One non-profit organization that fights modern slavery is the Not For Sale Campaign. The organization uses its Web site and online magazine to tell people how they can become anti-slavery activists. (Visit: www.notforsalecampaign.org)

Fighting oppression

In countries with oppressive or unjust governments, human rights violations happen every day. Human rights organizations keep records of these violations. They also pressure the violators to stop.

Downpressers

The Universal Declaration of Human Rights says everyone has the right to freedom of thought, **conscience**, and religion. People should not be thrown into jail or tortured because they disagree with their government or belong to a religious group the government opposes.

Make it stop

When people are detained, or placed in jail for their beliefs or actions, human rights activists often publicize the detainment. Their aim is to increase awareness and get more people to support them in trying to get the person released. The ultimate goal is to have freedoms granted to everyone. Often, this means educating people and telling them what their rights are or should be.

Activists call attention to China's oppression in Tibet by asking people to boycott the 2008 Olympic Games in Beijing. Part of their activism means shaming the oppressor publicly and making other people aware of human rights violations.

FREE THE PANCHEN LAMA

FREE! THE PANCHEN LAMA

Get Active!

BIG MOUTH

What is a prisoner of conscience?

A prisoner of conscience is someone who has been jailed because of their race, religion, skin color, beliefs, or lifestyle. Prisoners of conscience are also non-violent people and are often political prisoners. Political prisoners are people who are jailed for their political beliefs. The human rights group Amnesty International began identifying prisoners of conscience and fighting for their release in 1962. The organization won a Nobel Peace Prize in 1977 for campaigning against torture. Amnesty International continues to speak for prisoners of conscience who cannot speak for themselves.

Mind power

Activist Stephen Biko once said: "the most potent weapon in the hands of the **oppressor** is the mind of the oppressed." Biko fought for human rights and freedoms in South Africa during apartheid (1948-1990). Apartheid was a period of severe discrimination where people were segregated according to their race. Biko died in 1977 after being beaten while in detention in a police station.

Courage and confidence

Biko knew that one weapon in the fight against apartheid was making people aware of their rights as humans and encouraging bravery and confidence. He founded an organization for black students and set up a health clinic, a fund for political prisoners, and classes in literacy. His work as an activist made him a target. His death made him an **icon** of the struggle to end injustice.

Beijing 2008

GAME'S OVER FREE TIBET

Silence hurts

In some countries, when people speak out against oppression and injustice, they risk their lives. Still, they speak out because they have no choice. Doing nothing would make them a silent partner in oppression.

Speaking out can be risky

After activist Stephen Biko was killed while in police detention, his family and friends did not believe that he died from an accident. One friend, journalist Donald Woods, took pictures of Biko's body at the morgue. The pictures showed that he was beaten to death, and exposed the government lie. Woods was forced to leave South Africa in 1978 when he felt his own life was threatened, but he returned after apartheid ended.

It takes courage to speak out, but it helps if you have other people to back you up.

Field Notes:

Both Nelson Mandela and Mohandas Gandhi fought for freedom and human rights in their countries. They both spent time in jail because of their beliefs. Mandela spent 27 years in prison for being an activist. He later became the first black president of South Africa. Gandhi was imprisoned several times during his fight for justice in **colonial** India. Their courage and conviction helped other less prominent activists endure jail time, fear, and violence.

"I have fought against white domination, and I have fought against black domination. I have cherished the ideal of a democratic and free society in which all persons live together in harmony and with equal opportunities. It is an ideal which I hope to live for and to achieve. But if needs be, it is an ideal for which I am prepared to die." – from Nelson Mandela's speech at his 1964 Rivonia Treason Trial

Nelson Mandela

"When I despair, I remember that all through history the way of truth and love has always won. There have been tyrants and murderers and for a time they seem invincible, but in the end, they always fall—think of it, always." – Mohandas Gandhi on fighting oppression and keeping positive

Women's rights

Women make up half of the world's population. Yet, in many parts of the world women are denied basic human rights just because they are women.

Right to vote

The fight for women's rights everywhere began more than a century ago. Women did not have the right to vote. They were not considered citizens. In the United States, lawmakers finally gave women the right to vote in 1920 through the 19th Amendment or change to the Constitution. Activists had to campaign for many years. In Canada, women were only legally considered "persons" in 1929. Women fought hard for the right to vote, and their success helped activists fight for more rights for women. The struggle for women's rights continues, both in North America and throughout the world. Until women are considered truly equal everywhere, violence and discrimination against them will continue.

DECLARATION OF SENTIMENTS

When, in the course of human events,
it becomes necessary for one portion of the family of man
to assume among the people of the earth
a position different from that which they have hitherto occupied,
but one to which the laws of nature
and of nature's God entitle them,
a decent respect to the opinions of mankind requires
that they should declare the causes
that impel them to such a course.

We hold these truths to be self-evident:
that all men and women are created equal;
that they are endowed by their Creator
with certain inalienable rights;
that among these are life, liberty, and the pursuit of happiness;
that to secure these rights governments are instituted,
deriving their just powers from the consent of the governed—
Whenever any form of Government
becomes destructive of these ends,
it is the right of those who suffer from it to refuse allegiance to it,

In the United States, Elizabeth Cady Stanton wrote a "Declaration of Sentiments" in 1848. Based on the Declaration of Independence, Stanton's declaration laid out areas of inequality for women. It was one of the first documents to present women's rights as human rights.

Women's rights activists

Women's rights activists are people who believe in the equality of women. They do everything from push for equal pay for all, to raising funds and awareness of women's causes.

Women's rights activists protest violence against women.

This United States postage stamp commemorates the work of activists who fought for women's suffrage, or the right to vote.

Get Active!

Investigating inequality

Gender equality means equality between the sexes in all areas including access to education and jobs. What else does it mean? Ask your friends and family what gender equality means to them. Do some investigating of your own. Find out about women in other countries, how they live, and what rights they have. An organization that can help you with your research is MADRE. This organization works to support women's rights around the world. Write to them to ask how you can help. (Visit www.madre.org.)

Children's rights

The United Nations has written two documents declaring children's rights. In 1959, the Declaration of the Rights of the Child defined several basic rights for children. These include the right to grow up in a healthy way, the right to go to school, and the right not to be harmed or forced into work.

In some countries, children must work to support their families. This means they give up school and the chance at a better life.

More protection

The UN's Convention on the Rights of the Child, passed in 1989, was adopted by many countries around the world. This document went further than the 1959 declaration. It stated that children are human beings independent of their parents or guardians and that they have many rights. Some of those rights include the right to be protected from all forms of physical and mental violence and from poor care—even from their own families.

Human rights activists believe child labor exploits children. These children are often forced to work long hours in unhealthy conditions and for low wages.

NO CHILD LABOR

Children and the law

Many countries have laws to protect children from exploitation in workplaces by setting minimum ages for working. Many countries also have laws that state that children who have committed crimes should not be treated as adults by the courts or be forced into military service. In fact, the **International Criminal Court** considers enlisting or enrolling children under 15 into the military a **war crime**. Despite these and other laws, children are often easy targets for abuse. Activists work to protect children's rights and make people aware that children are not possessions that can be sold, bartered, or tossed away.

* BIG MOUTH

Get Active!

Investigating children's rights

Many human rights organizations monitor children's rights around the world. This means they investigate abuses and call for action. Some focus on one issue, such as children used as soldiers, or helping abused children in one country. The issues surrounding children's rights are so enormous and complex that activists sometimes concentrate on single issues instead of everything at once. Think about what issues are important to you, and use your local library and computer to do more research. If you would like to prevent child labor, for example, join an organization that fights to prevent it. Think about giving some of your allowance to this organization to help them.

Fighting genocide

Genocide means the killing of a group of people of the same race, religion, cultural or ethnic group, or nationality. People who carry out genocides intend to exterminate, or wipe out, an entire group of people. The term genocide was first used after World War II to describe the Holocaust. In 1948, the UN passed the Convention on the Prevention and Punishment of Genocide.

Genocide today

Despite laws, UN conventions, and international outrage, genocide still happens. Here are some shocking cases:

- In the south Asian country of Cambodia, an estimated two million people were murdered during a 1975 to 1979 genocide.
- In 1994, up to one million people were killed during the Rwandan Genocide in Africa. The killings took place over 100 days, while United Nations peacekeepers could do almost nothing to stop it.
- Today, the African country of Sudan is at the center of a genocide campaign. About 500,000 people have been killed or have died of starvation or disease, while trying to escape killing squads in the Darfur region.

Get Active!

Refugee camps

Many people who flee from the violence of genocide go to refugee camps. The camps provide safety, but they are often overcrowded and lack food and water. Help people in refugee camps by becoming an advocate. Educate yourself by reading about conflicts and genocides in the world. There are many Web sites set up by charities that assist refugees. Contact one of them—you may be able to help by raising funds or writing letters to newspapers or politicians.

Field Notes:

The efforts of one activist, lawyer Raphael Lemkin, forced the United Nations to recognize that mass killings against a specific group were a crime. Lemkin learned of the 1915 Armenian genocide as a teenager living in Poland. As an adult, 49 members of his family, including his parents, were murdered in the Holocaust. He wrote papers and worked to promote laws that guaranteed the rights of minority groups and to help prevent future genocides.

"Why should genocide be recognized as an international problem? Why not treat it as an internal problem of every country, if committed in time of peace, or as a problem between belligerents, if committed in time of war? The practices of genocide anywhere affect the vital interests of all civilized people. Its consequences can neither be isolated nor localized. Tolerating genocide is an admission of the principle that one national group has the right to attack another because of its supposed racial superiority..."
- Raphael Lemkin, Genocide — A Modern Crime, in Free World Magazine, April 1945

Public monuments and murals, such as this one in Italy protesting genocide in Sudan, are one way to make many people aware of human rights violations.

25

In the trenches

Human rights activists are ordinary people who do extraordinary things. The activists profiled here became involved at a young age.

Mahatma Gandhi

One of the world's best-known human rights activists was Mohandas (Mahatma) Gandhi. He fought for Indian independence from Britain in the 1940s using non-violent resistance. He never waivered in his belief that racism, prejudice, and **bigotry** must be countered with peaceful non-cooperation, strikes, and marches. He

Gandhi is thought of as the "father of the nation" in India.

spent time in jail for his activism, but his methods were successful. India gained independence in 1949. Many later activists used Gandhi's methods in their fight for human rights and justice.

Laura Hannant

When she was a child, Laura Hannant met one of her heroes, **humanitarian** and nun Mother Teresa. Laura wanted to help people just as her heroes did and became an advocate for children's rights. She was the first chairperson for the International Children's Jury which awards a world's children's prize for the rights of the child each year. Laura spoke to the Canadian parliament about children's rights. At 16, she gave a speech at the United Nations on the rights of children and how adults need to listen to them. Today, Laura still speaks out about children's rights as human rights.

Desmond Tutu

Desmond Tutu grew up in racially **segregated** South Africa. When he was a boy, a white man took off his hat and greeted his mother with respect. The action was unusual for that time, and Tutu was amazed. The man's actions influenced Tutu's beliefs about human rights in his

Desmond Tutu was a teacher and later an Anglican priest.

country during apartheid: that all humans had dignity. He spoke against apartheid and organized peaceful marches. In 1984, he was awarded the Nobel Peace Prize for his work. After apartheid ended in 1994, Tutu served as head of the Truth and Reconciliation Commission, a government commission which worked to unify the country by dealing with the human rights abuses committed during apartheid. A well-respected man, Tutu also used his influence in other human rights fights.

Stephanie Nyombayire

Stephanie Nyombayire was an eight-year-old living in the Republic of Congo with her parents in 1994 when she was told the genocide in Rwanda had claimed the lives of 100 of her relatives. Her grandparents and many aunts, uncles, and cousins had been murdered. Stephanie could not accept that nothing could have been done to prevent the genocide and save lives. Later, as a student at an American college, she formed the Genocide Information Network with six friends. The network tries to prevent genocide and human rights abuses by speaking out and encouraging young people to get involved in awareness and fundraising campaigns. Her group raises money for peacekeeping missions and to help refugees.

What you can do

Get together with friends to brainstorm ways you can help.

Change starts at home. Volunteer at your local nursing home or retirement home and learn how it feels to help people.

Some human rights activists become active because they experienced injustice first-hand. Others become involved because they do not want to silently witness human rights abuses. Fighting against abuses makes the world a better place for everyone.

Silence hurts

There are many ways to be a human rights activist. One of the most important ways of fighting injustice is to use your voice. Speaking out against oppression is a powerful way to help the oppressed. Activists also write, sing, dance, and make films to get word out.

Getting started

When an activist decides to take on a cause, they must be fearless and dedicated. It is important to only take on a cause that you feel strongly about because, if you don't care about the cause, how will you convince others to care and to make changes? This means learning all you can about the issue. Go to the library, watch the news, and investigate Internet sites on issues you are interested in. Keep files of information and don't be afraid to share them!

Group work

Joining a group or forming one of your own is another way to be an effective activist. The work can be distributed in a group. Some people can research and others can write letters to people in power asking them to get involved in a human rights issue. Groups can also help raise funds through events such as bake sales, garage sales, or concerts. Be creative in thinking of ideas to raise money or gain attention for your cause.

Organize a bake sale. Ask people to donate the food and give the proceeds to charity.

Get Active!

BIG MOUTH

Write a letter

Write a letter or e-mail the media or a politician. Tell them about your cause and why it is important. Ask them to help and give them suggestions on what they can do. If you are writing to the media, address your letter to the editor. When you write to the media, you want them to publicize your cause, or make it known to other people. Find out who your congressperson or member of parliament is. Member lists can be found at your library or online (www.congress.org in the United States and www.canada.gc.ca in Canada). They have the power to make laws that affect human rights in your country. They can also press for rights abroad.

Rights organizations

On this page, you will find Web sites of some well-known organizations that appear in this book. It is important that you view these sites with your teacher or parent. Some Web sites or links from these sites may contain topics and images of a sensitive nature. Discuss the information you read on these Web sites with your teacher or parent, and then make up your own mind about how you feel about the subject.

Human Rights Watch (HRW)

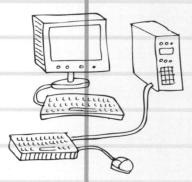

Human Rights Watch (HRW) is a *non-governmental organization (NGO)* that investigates human rights abuses throughout the world. It is the largest human rights organization in the United States but has offices around the world. HRW works with victims of human rights abuses and activists to expose abuses and hold people accountable for their actions. Human Rights Watch encourages schools to get involved in human rights issues. Their Web site contains a lot of information for human rights research, including reports on countries or governments that abuse human rights. Visit www.hrw.org.

Amnesty International (AI)

Amnesty International (AI) is a global human rights organization that researches human rights abuses and campaigns to stop them. In existence since 1961, AI has gained a reputation for helping prisoners of conscience. Their Web address is: www.amnesty.org.

MADRE

MADRE is an international women's human rights organization which works on peace and economic issues, combating violence against women, and women's health issues. MADRE's programs directly assist women in 11 different countries. Visit MADRE at www.madre.org.

The Carter Center

The Carter Center is a human rights organization started by former U.S. President Jimmy Carter and his wife Rosalynn. The center focuses on health issues and resolving conflicts. The center's Web address is: www.cartercenter.org.

UNICEF

The United Nations International Children's Emergency Fund (UNICEF) works for children's rights to basic education, health, and protection from violence. Their Web address is: www.unicef.org.

GET ACTIVE!

Glossary

advocate Someone who argues for a cause

barbaric Cruel and brutal

bigotry Intolerance toward people of another race or those who have different opinions

civil rights The rights of citizens to equality and social and political freedom

colonial Relating to a country or territory ruled by another country

conscience An inner voice or guide

degrading Something that is humiliating or causes loss of respect

detainment To keep someone in custody

dignity A sense of pride or self respect

discriminate Unjust treatment of someone based on race, sex, or age

Emancipation Proclamation An announcement made by U.S. President Abraham Lincoln in 1862 which freed all slaves

entitled A legal right or claim to something

evolve To develop gradually over time

exile Barred from one's country

exploite To use and benefit unfairly from someone else's work

Holocaust The mass murder of six million Jews by the German Nazis. Millions of other persecuted groups were also murdered during World War II

humanitarian Humane, charitable, or concerned with human welfare

icon A symbol of something

International Criminal Court A court that tries people for crimes against humanity such as genocide and war crimes

moral Concerned with what is right and wrong

non-governmental organization (NGO) An organization that helps people but is not part of a government

oppressor Someone who inflicts hardship on another

refugee Someone forced to leave their country to escape persecution

sanction A penalty or loss of reward, meant to help enforce a law

segregated Set apart or separated from others

Thirteenth Amendment An 1865 change to the U.S. constitution which officially abolishes and prohibits slavery

United Nations An international organization of countries established in 1945 to promote peace, security, and cooperation

war crime An action carried out during war that violates international rules of war

World War II An international war (1939-1945)

Index

Printed in China — CT